Snow at the

Liz McSkeane was born in Glasgow of Scottish and Irish parents and has lived in Dublin since 1981. She has worked as a teacher and broadcaster, and is now a freelance educational consultant specialising in curriculum development and educational disadvantage. She has a Masters degree in Education from the Open University. Her work in education and training has taken her to Central and Eastern Europe and in the more distant past, to France, Portugal and Spain.

She has pursued a parallel working life in writing, and in 1989 she was co-founder of *Acorn*, the Dublin Writers' Workshop journal, as well as co-facilitator of the workshop for two years. Her work has been published in magazines and journals in Ireland and the UK and in 1999, she won the Hennessy/*Sunday Tribune* New Irish Writer of the Year Award for her poetry.

Snow at the Opera House

Poems by
Liz McSkeane

**NEW
ISLAND**

Snow at the Opera House
First published July 2002
New Island Books
2 Brookside
Dundrum Road
Dublin 14

ISBN 1 902602 93 5

New Island receives financial support from The Arts
Council (An Chomhairle Ealaíon), Dublin, Ireland.

Cover image: Getty Images
Interior typesetting & cover design: New Island
Printed in Ireland by Colour Books Ltd.

Contents

⁂ Part One

Life Class 8

Artemis 9

Risk 10

The Morning After 11

All My Pretty Ones 12

Butterflies 13

Magpie 14

Reflection 15

Selective Perception 16

Sinking 18

In the Attic 19

Safe-keeping 20

Cold Turkey 21

Dream 22

⁂ Part Two

Saturday, Five Past Three 24

Strategies 25

Plea Bargain 26

On Daring to Speak the Truth 28

Survivor 29

A Young Man Has Been Sentenced to Death 30

Vegetable 31

Turlough 33

Steps 34

Nude 35

Snap! 36
Law of the Lever 37
On the Possibility of Reconstruction 39
At Harlech Castle 41
In Flight 42
Samsara 43

✳ Part Three

Sculpture, Botanic Gardens 46
Provenance 47
Vertigo 49
Other 50
Magnum Opus 51
Zola's Photographs 52
In Franz Liszt's Place 53
Un-named 56
Invitation 57
Getting a Fix on Reality 59
Water Lilies, Botanic Gardens 60
Women in the Gellért Baths 61
Snow at the Opera House 63

Acknowledgements 64

Part One

Life Class

The teacher says, forget the outlines, try
for depth in shadings to catch the tension
of suppressed movement and dimensions
you don't see. Politics of the body.
I just don't get it. I half-close my eyes
and the whole thing shifts to a new version,
another meaning. Tricks of perception
like this bother me, make me doubt what I
see: I can't tell how things should be looked at,
interpreted, pinned down. The outlines
give me trouble starting with the skin
then the space we have to negotiate
between my standpoint and yours, what defines
where my boundaries end and yours, begin.

Artemis

Love, or a certain kind of love
or even the lack of it, is hardly the point
but rather
what you are prepared to do to get it
and then, to hang on to it.

I've done it myself – abandoned
the forest, put down my bow.
Immersed myself.
This love of yours is a full-time job,
it wears me out.

Here, where it's quiet and green
I find things to look at and think about, wild
things to be tamed. Others, I let roam free.
I pursue the goals I choose, without compulsion.
I seek no followers.

She, on the other hand, has got it in
for anyone who thinks
they might be able to do without her.
She's convinced she makes the world go round
(as if there were only one kind of birth!)

Yet those who manage to catch sight of me swear
I am covered, just covered! all over, with breasts.

Risk

is a wedding in Chinese

when opportunity and danger wrap
limbs together and stoneheavy drop
on small creatures at pasture or wing-beat
unison above the cloud-line, beyond sight

not a lone dancer on the brink
courting the push from behind.

The Morning After

That breath is just a breath;
those stirrings, manoeuvres on the borders
of repose, that's all. Pale light
slips across the quilt, trails questions:
In what language are you dreaming?
It's early, very early,
much too soon to waken, time
yet for another hour's sleep.

All My Pretty Ones

Sometimes, in a café or on the beach
or any place they're gathered in a bunch
your face could be Macduff's – stricken,
a study in tenderness and loss and lack
of comprehension – when he gets the news
and always, the moment you turn back
to the talk: the rustle of leaves, the crack
of a twig. A forest draws near.

Butterflies

Everyone else seems to love them.
They give me the creeps – all that fluttering,
delicate beauty, it's so in-your-face
there's no getting away from it, no
possibility of defence.

Is it true that it's all only dust?
The mottles, the speckles, the lovely
mother-of-pearl variegation,
just brushed on and just as easily brushed
off? That if you do that to one, it dies?

See what I mean? You don't even
have to trample on one by accident
or tear a wing while flapping it away
from your eyes. A flick of a finger's
enough to do it, a whisper

of a breath that doesn't buy the *Love me!*
Admire me or I'll break! routine.
That's what's really in room One-O-One,
not rats or cockroaches but bits
of gorgeousness and no windows.

Magpie

Something is there. I'm sure. I sense it first
then hear a rustle coming from our bedroom.
Still I hesitate, expecting the worst
and open the door on half-spread wings, a tomb-
etched profile, one unblinking eye that tracks
me as I hug the wall. He shivers, backs
into the grate when I fling the window
open. I can't just leave and hope he'll go
away – the mess, shit, feathers, blood – so I
call again for you. You grab him, all bones
and wild heart-pulse except none of it shows
in your face and I breathe *don't die, don't die*.
I turn when you throw him skywards. Don't let
me know if he made it or not, not yet.

Reflection

I saw one today
garlic-draped
complete with wooden stake
and a crucifix
hell-bent on dispensing
salvation

and noticed only
much later
tell-tale punctures
on the lily-white
of the neck
breath on hair
whispered
Come on, baby
just another
little
drop

the image is fading
there's a sharpness now
in what's left of the smile
kind of a red look
in the eye

Selective Perception

I'm wondering what colour's black today.
(I'm sure when you decide you'll let me know.)
From where I'm standing, looked at in this light
it definitely seems – well – rather black.
But then, what's there may not be what I see.
It wouldn't be the first time I've been wrong.

It's not so much about who's right (and wrong)
as who's most suitably equipped: broad day-
light shows up grey for people who don't see
certain colours. Some see none at all. They know
colour exists, we say so and though black
looks clear they lack the necessary light

receptors to perceive all shades of light
and dark. Does this mean what they see is 'wrong'?
What if they got together, argued black
was white, conducted all their day-to-day
business accordingly? Would we *know*
they were different from us in how they see?

And would it matter? Probably. To see
that others view things in a different light –
one group of South Sea Islanders we know
about who don't see colours ask 'what's wrong
with that?' – is one thing. To live with it, day
in day out, you saying 'white' and me, 'black'

is something else, like living in a black-
out or on two different islands. We see
each other, wave, guess who's meaning what today
and it's not just a question of light
and dark and shades of grey. I wish. What's wrong
is, we just don't agree on what we know

is real lately. I'm sure – I think I know –
something's amiss. 'Watch out for the big black
iceberg. If I've got the colour wrong
let's swap impressions: how do you see
it?' 'What iceberg? Where? That's just a trick of light!'
Experience will tell. If we should some day

sink, well then we'll know: that what I did see
was, if not quite black, then dangerous; that light
won't make right wrong; but will turn night to day.

Sinking

There may be other life-boats but I think not –
none with a place for me. A young man offers
me assistance, my sister looking on.
Everyone is waiting to see what I will do,
if I will make her two young children motherless –
I, not yet needed, barely twenty – or restore
her to them. O, if only they would close
the gate against me as they have locked the Irish
from the deck, say what they really mean! But no.
It is I who must deny myself this last chance
to be saved, my next act to be determined
by breeding and good manners. Now my sister
does not look at me. Had I even one child
and she two, or I two and she four,
would this make her life worth the double of mine?
Or does the very state of motherhood confer
value which I cannot claim? How will they
remember me? *Young woman, not yet twenty,*
childless. Drowned, a heroine.

In the Attic

Who the hell does Rochester think he is?
Keeping me locked up here with the barest
of sustenance and no-one but whey-faced
Grace for company? She brings more than food,
she gives me information, takes pleasure
in what she imagines is my distress.
Some nights I see them for myself – that grey
ninny with her plain dresses and parched lips
minding her *p*'s and *q*'s, doing her best
to entertain him without seeming to,
assuring him she plays – o! but a little! –
careful to keep her cleverness to herself.
Some nights I spy on her while she's undressing
in that damp room they gave her with the narrow
bed and mildewed sheets and watch her practise
doe-eyed in her looking-glass and touch herself.
Her arms are thin but something flickers
still, something darts out in those pert answers
of hers – he does not care too much for them –
yet he may be fascinated by a spark
if he's got the kindling of it. I blaze
unbidden, don't do *doe-eyed* so I'm up here
and she's with him. What's more, be sure, she knows
of me – that I exist, that he's afraid,
his shame. She's just decided not to know.
And what of Grace? What's her advantage
in keeping me here? Money? Sheer devotion
from the perfect servant who knows her station?
Whatever. You couldn't do it without them,
all those women, keeping you safe from me.
You're underestimating me again.
I'm on my way, downstairs, to warm you up.

Safe-keeping

How about:
'Because (I think I'm right) the contract
states *the principal must be repaid in full* –
no more than that – which seemed to call for a discreet
approach, the canny eye of a custodian
to guarantee a fair return, not some whizz-kid
who'd promise you the moon and in the morning steal
the eye out of your head. Because myself, I tend
towards *understatement,* nothing flash, that's not my style
besides which, for the most part I have found no need
of high-risk strategies to, shall we say, muddle
by quite nicely. And in these parts to parade
one's assets, well, it's not the thing as you, above all
have ample cause to know . . . no sooner raise your head
over the battlements, etcetera! Because
I genuinely thought the best use – you say "hoard",
I should rather say "safeguard" – of such a pittance
was in fact accomplished: namely, reimbursement
of the full amount, no more, it's true but no less
either. To *strut your stuff* and *if you've got it, flaunt
it*'s fine if you've also got the back-up – money
in the family, for instance. Did you really want
to come back here, review accounts and hear me say
"Sorry, the cupboard's bare, just thought I'd have a little
flutter with your two-and-fourpence, lost it but hey,
who's counting?" What would you have said to that? And while
we're at it, might a spot of credit not be due
for prudence? That cannot be too much to ask . . . . '
                                                                    Well?
Not bad. I'd skip the you above all plus the two
and fourpence but the rest is fine, unanswerable.

Cold Turkey

The other day, so unobtrusively
I barely noticed, anger left and since
the agitation's gone this vacancy
is bothering me. Living's less intense
when rage burns out, there's too much life to fill.
I miss the turbulence, the highs and lows
that make you feel alive. Just being still
takes practice. Deprives you of a purpose.
Like red meat, anger over-stimulates
the senses. It creates an appetite
for spice and anything more delicate –
like peace, for instance – tastes too bland, too slight
to sharpen up perceptions that can't see
the point of getting used to being free.

Dream

It goes like this: my mother and I
just back from his funeral
exhausted and wept out from the grave
and the whole of the year before.
We open the front door and there he is
looking, not well but definitely, alive.
He smiles gently, a bit sheepish
as if sorry for having given us
all that trouble and explains
that it was all a big mistake,
some kind of a nightmare – he never died,
was never buried and here he is back
with us for a while and we all rejoice
until it dawns on me that some day,
probably quite soon, we'll have to go through
the whole thing again and this time
it will be for real.

I think it might be an omen of something big;
a warning, not to count on anything;
a challenge, something like *Don't start
anything you can't follow through on*
and *Are you sure you're up to this?*
*Because this isn't the stuff you get in pop songs
or drone on about in poems,
this is for grown-ups and may include
desperation as one way or another,
all things pass*; a wake-up call,
not to strategies or self-defence
but a call to surrender –
to life, to the real thing, to love.

*
**

Part Two

Saturday, Five Past Three

Whether one or a few of them ever
threw a stone on, say, the Garvaghy
Road, sang the Sash or the Broad Black Brimmer,
fucked the Pope/the Queen, told us that *tiocfaidh
ár lá,* read their Catechism or King
James didn't seem to figure which means if
I or you want to get that *Je Reviens*
she likes, some cans of Harp and 7-Up
to bring tonight, not necessarily
from the Omagh branch of Boots the Chemist
and neighbouring off-licence but any
other one, Jervis Street maybe, that next
year at five past three we could hear our own
silence, two minutes', spliced in the genome.

Strategies

Panic batters at my sleep,
hovers, beats on the window
like a crazy drum, pauses,
a dry scraping on glass.

I can't bear the struggle –
wings fluttering in my cupped hand
or crushed between finger and thumb.
I turn over again, searching for rest.

Lamplight spills to the floor.
On a dark Belfast street I hail
a taxi. *Round here you'd better
phone for one* the locals say.

Whirring butterfly wings
throb the sky, an invisible
warbird caught in a sheet of cloud.
It palpitates, fades. There's no way
through.

I'm afraid to sleep now.
Tomorrow, I know, broken
wings will litter my window
or in the night brush my eyes,
my lips.

Plea Bargain

If we were dogs, they'd shoot us.
Wild dogs, or dogs gone mad, or wounded dogs.
They'd shoot them.

They won't shoot us.

They're pointing guns at us, but not to shoot us with.
The guns are to stop us from running away.
The five of us, lined up, waiting.
Do you see those sticks there,
leaning on the side of the barn?
They're for us.
That's how they'll do it.

They won't waste their bullets, on us.

This is how it happens, this is what I've seen:
some of them get frightened, after the first blow;
they think they'll want to, or that they'll like it
but after the first blow they see
and they get frightened
because they're still human beings, after all,
and so are we and that's what they see
when they strike for the first time;
but they can't go back because something's done
and it seems impossible to go on, but they must.
So they panic.
Quite often, they panic, and that makes them clumsy.
The more they want to finish you off, for it to be over,
the clumsier they get and the more they can't
because you won't, you just won't
and you get more broken and more broken
and sometimes they're screaming themselves, as much
as you are and if they scream long enough

26

they might get to like it after all,
which is good
because it's over quite quickly then.

Why do we let them? Keep us here, waiting,
with their pointed guns?
If we took them on (I could do it myself)
they'd have to use the bullets
and it would be that much easier.
But I don't think I will. Not now.
It's too certain –
a quick end, yes, but definitely
an end. The other way –
well, you never know.
Help might come, even at the very last minute.
It might. It could.
So I will wait, until they start
and you will wait and we won't know
if help ever did arrive, until after
the last blow has fallen.
That is, never.

On Daring to Speak the Truth

that most – not all, but enough – of what was supposed
   to have been forgotten
               is remembered
that the meaning of what is remembered
                      is understood
that some of this will never
         be forgiven

that it is sometimes too late
that already it is too late
that some things can never be undone

that silence is a weapon of the oppressor
that the cost of silence is the loss of the voice
that silence is an instrument of self-mutilation
         and eventually, suicide

that for some things, there can be no possible explanation
   or justification
that ignorance and pain are no defence
that attack is the best means of attack

that truth-telling, once potentially fatal,
   now is merely highly dangerous
        and therefore, necessary

Survivor

You meet her in the ruins
of a silent city
where sunlight glances on bones
and the wind carries whispers of the dead.

You coax her with these gifts:
a glittering star –
she shrinks from it;
your songs –
she stops her breath;
this box of paints –
she chooses crimson
makes a jagged circle
two torsos
a pair of severed heads.

A Young Man Has Been Sentenced to Death

A young man has been sentenced to death.
He has killed a swan, perhaps many.
He is beautiful.
His hair shines golden in the sunlight.

He is brought on a final pilgrimage,
perhaps to see the places of his crimes.

I am sure that the sentence will be commuted.
His crime was great, it is true. He deserves
punishment for the killing of swans.
He does not deserve to die.

I am sure that the sentence will be commuted.

One approaches from behind,
extended hand flat –
rigid as an axe
waiting to descend.

He is executed with a blow
to the back of his golden neck.
He falls.

There is immeasurable sadness.

Vegetable

I see stars, sometimes.
I think they're stars, sparks
shooting through the darkness
making the black more black.

Maybe they're not stars.
Maybe it's not seeing.
Maybe it's pain,
what pain would be, or used to be.

I remember pain
and something else
the way an amputated limb is remembered
as an absence
except that there is nothing else,
nothing to do the remembering.

What is this I,
anyway? All there is
is this
limitlessness.
Nothing, no one to touch.
Nothing with which to touch.
Only this blackness
or rather, those pins of stars.
If it weren't for the stars
I wouldn't know the dark was there.
I wouldn't know that I was there:
with nothing to catch on to,
these thoughts would fade.

Are these thoughts? Is that what they are?

Is that what I am?

Sometimes, something shifts.
How do I know this?
I can't tell.
Perhaps it's not movement at all,
perhaps it's a sound –
a small animal, scurrying;
someone shovelling earth
or planting a flower.

Does this happen often? I wonder
How can I know what often is?
It happens.
Enough to remind me
that I am here
or, if there is no here,
that I am, that I am.

What if I were to be snuffed out?
Is this possible?
And if so, how might it happen?

I want to be snuffed out.
If this is seeing, I want not to see.

I don't mean that.
Those shades of darkness, those different
shades of blackness.
Those shifts. That flower.
Things change.
Things do change.

Turlough

For now, there's just this one, staring eye
of black water set in a limestone
skull. I'm on the edge looking in

where dead rushes fringe the lakeside.
There's no sky to speak of. Reflections
vanish, it's the opaque sheen of thin

ice. Soon, though, when the rains
stop, the waters will fall, sucked
back to the centre. Strange growths

will appear in the cracks, things that really
shouldn't be here. Gentian, Edelweiss.
God knows what else. And the lake will be gone,

its socket raw, dried, bared to the sun.

Steps

ten stone steps cut into a hole in the ground

at my feet
                (this is what really bothers me)
your black shoes polished bright as they never were
as if you'd left something important behind

maybe I'll step into them see where they lead
or maybe I'll toss them clattering after you
if I dare
                it's their blackness, perfect blackness
stops me dead
                instead I stare into a hole
counting ten stone steps

and puzzle over your forgotten footwear

Nude

Imperfect circle of sorrow she sits
curving a broken arc
of flattened buttocks and parted thighs.
Her arms embrace one knee
and cradle her drooping head.

Her body bathes in shadow.
It would swallow her but for
a whip of light gashing
one shoulder and the bold,
unbroken line defining her.

Caught in the fulcrum of despair
she rocks sorrow to sleep
and balancing on the blue earth,
cleaves an abyss before her.

Snap!

The camera flashes, like a perfect eye
which captures all that's needed to preserve
a faithful image of reality,

to lay out evidence we can't deny,
hard facts you've gathered. With that steady nerve
(and camera flashes, like a perfect eye)

you cast light not only on *what* but *why*
and how much sympathy they all deserve.
A faithful image of reality

which I don't see myself must just rely
on you or him or people who observe
those camera flashes. Like a perfect eye

trained on the object which will simplify
the picture you record – you must disturb
this faithful image of reality

by being there as I do when my
gaze collapses waves, persuades photons to swerve
and camera flashes like a perfect eye
create an image of reality.

Law of the Lever

*Give me a lever and a place to stand and I will move
the earth*

                                        Archimedes

It works.

Take this: a massive weight. Call it
the State, apparently unbudgeable.
Then, puny us.
It's all so far away, so huge,
it seems impossible to move
anything, anywhere.

The trick: to make the distance work;
to use a smaller weight –
a strike, an unarmed rally – to shift
a big one.
Then, when things start to accelerate
there may be moments when it could go
either way but with a bit of nerve
and luck there's slippage
and the mass of power starts to tilt
and favour us.

It all hinges on how the energy
is parcelled out:
nothing will disappear, nothing is new,
it all just moves around. Simple.
Egyptian engineers knew this
and whoever built Stonehenge.
Plus, what you gain in one place
must be lost to somewhere else.

Already, far beyond the mountains –

Montenegro? Kosovo? –
some guy waving a stick around
is stirring it. He's yelling all
he needs now is a bit of space.
He thinks he's going to change the world.

On the Possibility of
Reconstruction

A postcard. Warsaw, nineteen forty-four,
the Old Town Square. Piles of sun-bleached stones –
before. Alongside, now. X, I am here –
after: gilded turrets, freshly-stencilled walls
and crooked roofs, a Disney set for Grimms'

exactly as it was five centuries
ago yet barely fifty years old,
a freeze-frame that recreates a showcase
time and place, managing to look solid
and, from this distance, all of a piece.

A cellar-café, tables in the sun.
A young man takes my order, disappears
underground into a mini-dungeon –
People like him, dragged out of bunkers like this
Two hundred thousand dead civilians

My guidebook shows five versions of the frontiers
of the country since the twenties – some bits
the neighbours swallow up or spit out, boundaries
shifting from one decade to the next
definitively re-drawn, a place fixed

now, forever, on the map of Europe
(from which it vanished, two centuries ago).
New faces are built, old ones get the nip
and tuck. Can anything so thoroughly blown
away ever be made completely whole?

It must be lodged in the DNA,
that drive to find a way out of the ruins,
to excavate them. To start again, to lay
new foundations from old plans, from no plans.
If this is possible, anything is.

At Harlech Castle

By now a portcullis would have barred
the way back and another crashed down ahead
of where I'm standing at the barest hint
that anyone unwelcome or who didn't
have a reason to be there, was there
unless it was routine and all comers
got the third degree. But I don't think so.
I imagine guards conferring. Do we know
you? State your business, show your references.
Bars dangle overhead, not obvious
to the visitor until you find
yourself hemmed in a narrow passage, blind
in the solid rock. I imagine
a moment or three of doubt. Do I want in
this much? And if it's not all it's cracked
up to be, from here there's no way back
to market days, the cottage, kids playing
in the dunes, a white-sailed boat heading
for the Irish coast and you'd have to ask
yourself if everything that got you past
the gate-house door was not a massive waste
of time, if all that energy was misplaced
and different choices might have led you
somewhere with a consistently better view,
decisions not quite made or planned but more
found, say. Encountered. Way to go.

In Flight

The air shivers to a faint keening
as the flock wheels into sight

so low and close that every beating
wing counts time to the eerie chorus

of eddies and swirls, each bird held
so, a perfect wingspan apart

steel-strung to an ancient radar
drawn northwards over rooftops, unfurled

on the snow-heavy sky scrolling
figures of eight until the arc grows

an arrow-head and the tail curves,
yields to formation, trails a few

stragglers on the wing-tips skirting
edges of flight, the destination.

Samsara

A transformation, but not quite: last night's
snow has covered lawns and pathways, whitened
shrubs and cedars to a thickness that quiets
footsteps and stills the voice. I'm unsettled
and at the same time, comforted, the way
the usual can be made to disappear
so easily. Sounds from the city fade
as if there's nothing left out there to hear.
I could stay here for a while, but as
the thought occurs to me I know I won't –
I can't take all this peace, it touches
something in me, leads me somewhere I don't
recognise. I must get back to what I know:
streets, people, coffee. Traffic. Melting snow.

Part Three

Sculpture, Botanic Gardens

Someone has built a tepee, of all things,
between the bluebell field and daffodils,
a shaky-looking tripod of saplings
held together with twine that should topple
at any minute. It's got a rootedness,
though, that's confident as a young tree,
each part in balance. I love the skewedness
of it and the slap-dash harmony
that mixes permissiveness and care
in just the right amounts: enough attention
to give it shape and make it hold its centre
but not too much, no search for perfection
or even symmetry in it, but freedom
to grow to itself, from its own wisdom.

Provenance

Some of the songs I got from home.
That last one came from my mother.
You can find a lot in your own
back yard if you take the bother
to look. Some, you have to search for
elsewhere. We had a lot of our
tunes from a man outside the town
and I know of a woman down
near Muckish, strangers visit her
and all she'll say before she starts
is *if I've got the air, it's yours,
I'll give it to you*. I've never
been to her but that's what they say,
I know. It often works that way.
And then again maybe you'd go
off nowhere in particular
and sometimes you won't even know
you're looking but you are and you're
listening, so you'll recognise the note
when you hear it and you'll know it
yourself, what's yours for the storing,
the turning over and passing
on. For it's not as though you own
it, after all and where's the sense
in hoarding? You give it out and once
in a while, once in a blue moon
if you're lucky it brings the house
down but you can't sit back for that's
never the end of it. They might
just have been in exceptional
form on that particular night
was all it was; or else you'll
never find a better song or be
in as good a voice. Some agree,

others say they weren't listening
anyway, meaning, you're wasting
your breath. That's when you have to know,
whatever it is that you've got
wherever it's from, that it's not
someone else's dressed up for show;
whoever it was that the tune
came from, who's doing the singing
is new.

Vertigo

When you think about it, it must have been a long shot,
that transition from four legs to two.
Thumbs made all the difference, I believe:
had it not been for thumbs, hands wouldn't have become
so useful and we'd have gone on using them
to balance while we snuffled the ground.
But here we are, erect and tall,
busy twiddling fingers, every skull
fairly packed with cortex, more than we know what
to do with. Unless you're Einstein or a London
cabbie and need to negotiate complex
universes. And if you don't, what can you make
with it all, for example if you've no intentions
regarding the shortest distance from the sun
to planet Earth or from Piccadilly to Notting Hill,
will any of it help with the vertigo
that comes from standing upright, and still?

Other

You're not really me, you know –
just somewhere where the real me lives,
less a machine than a suit of clothes which I
(whatever that is) put on for a while,
which requires some basic care from time
to time, a task which ghostly I
take lately more and more to heart.

Your image is all over:
in shadows flickering on cave walls,
in various loose parts –
an eye here, a breast there – all with a purpose
and also cleverly, meaning something else.
You've never measured up
though to be fair, you've never let me down

so far. One day you will.
One day you'll turn against me
or give in to something bigger than both of us
or even just quietly wear out
which leaves me wondering how there'd be a me
without a you. One day, I know, you'll leave me

high and dry.

Magnum Opus

from the Burrell Collection, Glasgow

Something about this Chinese earthenware
two-handled vessel, third millennium
BC perplexes me: beneath the rim,
two tiny holes the potter's taken care
to hide. Why? And what were they meant for?
So that a twist of horsehair could be tied firm,
laced through and slung across the farmer's arm
to carry water to the fields? Remember,
in the Sauchiehall Street Habitat,
those dark-on-russet soup bowls with the fish
motif, I thought I'd wait a while and see –
some other time – a woman hesitate,
stoop, read: *glazed earthenware two-handled dish,*
north Europe, third millennium, AD

Zola's Photographs

His dog, propped up on its master's knee, looks
into the lens. People on bicycles –
a boy, both feet on the handlebars, whoops
downhill. Early morning: wind rattles
the milk-cans on their cart. Barges on the Seine.
Paris in the snow. His little daughter,
posing. Older, glares: *papa, not again!*
A pile of books. Bits of the Eiffel Tower.
Zola in a suit, reclining on a chaise
longue, flivells a copy of *L'assommoir*.
And Jeanne in her chemise, shoulders bare, half-
ready, turns towards the camera, gaze
unsmiling, steady, fingering her hair.
People didn't then, not for a photograph.

In Franz Liszt's Place

Starting with his bedroom, spacious
and high-ceilinged, off Andrassi
út, beyond a sweep of gracious
marble stairs and two oak doors – I see
a lot to dwell on, here: his single
bed piled high, Hungarian-style,
with pillows, arranged to show
that he was rich; a piano
which once belonged to Beethoven;
at least two versions of his name –
Ferenc at home and Franz when fame
in other countries beckoned. Here, in
Liszt's apartment, unmissable,
the images on every wall,
in pencil drawings, etchings, Liszt
in charcoal, watercolour, oils,
a couple of grand portraits, his
profile cast in bronze medallions;
Liszt the youth, with long, fine hair that drapes
the haughty angles of his face;
many of the man matured, crowned
with success; in middle age, jowled
and stately, all the way to old
age and all the while, carrying
with him his younger self, wearing
traits which slackened skin and lines re-mould,
obscure, but don't obliterate:
his character, shown in a state
of dignity. All these fragments
of key moments in his time must
add up to something whole, like remnants
you'd combine, make an essence
out of, so that you could see
it all, complete. Remember how we

used to play with picture cards, stack
them, flick the bundle front to back
quite slowly – you'd see the figures
move. We could do that with him, get
them moving fast enough to let
change show but not so fast that years
become invisible, meaningless
in the chronology; or else
we could arrange his portraits, all
faded to translucent images,
in one tall pile which we could call
the *whole*, where each one finishes
all the others and vice versa,
definitive, we'd say, *here's a
composite version of a life
which carries within it the strife
and joy of years, shown on this face.*
Shouldn't that be possible?
To sum up the inevitable
as if it had been, like a race
that would only ever have one
ending, but still, had to be run?
Unless it's been done already.
Perhaps it has. Perhaps in each
image his face hints at what may be,
shows a draft of what he'll reach,
as well as carrying what went
before. And now myself, intent
on keeping track, peers back at me.
I take a closer look and see
a few lines, new-ish, not there long
enough to go unnoticed
and owned, as faces are in photos
of near-strangers who belong
forever to one moment. Yet
they don't, for others. Others get
their continuity the way

you get your own, your lover's, friends'
mother's, in a long, unrolling day
you barely notice till it's over,
although you see them with their past,
with possibilities for next
week, next year, not realising
what this is: a kind of making.
Then there's the dead, immobilised
with luscious, never-greying hair
while almost all you can remember
is the end, the rest deleted
as if what came in those last
months was all there'd been: a shadow cast
on everything that went before.
That's what makes it so important
to fuse the bits into a more
representative, coherent –
something. To restore a balance,
make sure the highs don't dazzle us
and the lows don't darken everything.
That's what's so great about being
great: armies of historians,
scholars, all trying to weigh Liszt
up, figure him out, put the gist
of him into a museum –
his old apartment – nothing else
required, to make of him such total, perfect, sense!

Un-named

This one appeals – greyish-purple water
spilled on stone. The next, streaked red. A rib-cage
dipped in blood? Débris of a slaughter?
The title should correct whatever image
I've formed of it, no doubt it's something else.
Turns out the title's in Hungarian
so no assistance there, just me, the canvas
and Sigmar Polke who, I guess, did mean
something by it especially as it's got
a name which isn't just *Untitled*. I
give up trying to figure out the rest, jot
down the artist's name wondering why
I'm always carrying my passport
around, when I could so easily lose it.

Invitation

We recognised him at once
although he was much changed
(the degradations of gaol
and hard labour have crushed him).
He looked up as we entered
from the terrace of the *rue du Bac*,
his eyes a question we took
for permission to join him.

He stood, while we threaded a path
between waiters clattering trays
and bottles, steering *plats
du jour* and glasses of *vin blanc*.
Eyes glittering, he gripped my hand
and kissed my wife, glancing
in the mirror like a nervous girl
when we ordered coffees and cognac.

He is long past vanity, alas,
though he still spreads his hands
(badly-calloused, now) as a king
spreading treasures before his subjects;
and his conversation is amusing
enough, still, to grace a London
dinner-table. Only once
did he ask for news of home
and as he whispered his inquiry,
his voice failed him.

When we rose to make another
rendezvous he lost composure,
fumbling in his waistcoat pocket,
protesting as I insisted
and when I turned, he had sunk

back in the worn velvet seat,
taking pains to lean out of the glare
of hissing gas-lamps, yet smiling
towards the terrace of the *rue du Bac*
perhaps hoping for a chance
encounter with an old acquaintance
who might invite him to coffee and cognac.

Getting a Fix on Reality

Apparently, Beuys loved the Irish light.
Artists do. The indeterminacy
of rain- and mist-blurred lines, the subtlety
of tones, appeal to them. The indefinite
invites interpretation – what might,
what could, what should – a lack of clarity
that shades our speech as well, less obviously,
words changing meaning to their opposite
like 'no' that fades to 'yes'. We're famous
for it: just when you think you might have grasped
what's going on, the sense evaporates.
Everything's clear until the wind changes,
then, nothing is. Then, you make it up. Or guess.

Water Lilies, Botanic Gardens

It's early days.
The leaves float thick,
covering the surface of the lake,
each cluster centred by a lily-pod
big as a plover's egg
full to bursting,
ripening to stars –
vermilion, white.
In a week or two they'll split open,
spill out onto the dark green,
daubs of vermilion, purple, white.

On the Yangtze river
the water lily leaves are strong,
so strong
a grown man can sit on them.

Women in the Gellért Baths

The light is the first thing you notice –
like dusk, though it's early morning
because of the windows, set so high
in the vaulted roof that the sun
sends shadows along and down the walls.
A turquoise mosaic cavern.
Two ovals of cobalt water.
My feet slap over polished granite
when I walk through the atrium
to the showers where I hesitate,
shiver a little in my black
one-piece which I peel off
before stepping into the pool,
to join the women of the Gellért baths.
Women standing, motionless, thigh-high
in the warm spring. Women squatting.
Women floating in it. Some women
sitting on the edge, feet submerged,
others wading, choosing their way
carefully, so as not to disturb.
Our bodies glisten. Skin puckers, soaks.
No-one speaks. Now and then someone sighs.
We're washing the world away, from breasts,
our firm, high breasts, our dark-nippled breasts,
our breasts that droop with age; from thighs, too,
dimpled and scrawny and from buttocks
and hair and bellies and all the rest
you see here, bared, unremarkable.
I close my eyes. It's said these waters
cleanse, heal, even, that the Turks knew
it and sank wells into the Danube rock
under Buda Hill. They could be right.
You could make peace, sign treaties here.
No-one would raise a hand or a voice.

It's Saturday morning. No-one does.
I float, chin-deep, how long I don't know
and when I stand up the sun has moved.
I wade, carefully, to the edge
in search of my swimsuit, noticing
nothing in particular. Unless,
our variousness. Or perhaps
the marvel of us, of us all.

Snow at the Opera House

They're serving coffee in the marbled hall.
At the other end glass balcony doors
reflect the chandeliers, the vast mirrors
in golden frames. Beyond, it's night. Snow
falls. Light spills over the parapet
and out there, four lamps cast an aura
that shows every flake, tumbling in perfect
rhythm with the rest into the lighted arc
then out of it again, fading back
into darkness to blend with all the others
and finally settle. I rest
my forehead on the cold of the windowpane
and clasp my cup. It warms me through the woollen
gloves and for a short while this is more
than just one person heavy with dampness
seeping through boots and too many sweaters,
that as well but getting ready not to be,
with the brightness of the lamps, the soft dark
of the night out there, the scent of coffee, the *A*
that's gathering in from the discord of strings
and flutes and the rest, calling us together,
in the few minutes that it takes to finish
my coffee, all this is contained. And the snow
falling, falling.
I will never forget it.
Now, it's not quite spring and the snow is long gone
but something of its quality remains:
an awareness of moments
as separate
like snowflakes that fall,
gather, settle into something else
and seem to disappear.

Acknowledgements

Acknowledgements are due to the following publications, where some of these poems first appeared: *Acorn, The Irish Times, Pandora's Box, Poetry Ireland Review, The Sunday Tribune.*